Start to Finish
Second Series

FROM Tree TO Paper

● PAM MARSHALL

LERNER PUBLICATIONS ⟩ Minneapolis

Lerner Publications Company
A division of Lerner Publishing Group, Inc.
241 First Avenue North
Minneapolis, MN 55401 USA

For reading levels and more information, look up this title at www.lernerbooks.com.

Photo Acknowledgments
The images in this book are used with the permission of: © iStockphoto.com/DNY59, p. 1; © Digital Vision/Getty Images, p. 3; © Inga Spence/Visuals Unlimited, Inc., p. 5; © iStockphoto.com/Josef Mohyla, p. 7; © Tom Thulen/Alamy, p. 9; © David R. Frazier Photolibrary, Inc./Alamy, p. 11; © Tips Images/SuperStock, pp. 13, 19; © RIA Novosti/Photo Researchers, Inc., p. 15; © Sally A. Morgan; Ecoscene/CORBIS, p. 17; © Bloomberg/Getty Images, p. 21; © Michael Wildsmith/Taxi/Getty Images, p. 23.

Front cover: © iStockphoto.com/Borut Trdina.

Main body text set in Arta Std Book 20/26.
Typeface provided by International Typeface Corp.

Library of Congress Cataloging-in-Publication Data

Marshall, Pam.
    From tree to paper / by Pam Marshall.
        p.   cm. — (Start to finish, second series.
    Everyday products)
        Audience: Grades K to 3.
        Includes bibliographical references and index.
        ISBN 978-0-7613-9184-5 (lib. bdg. : alk. paper)
        ISBN 978-1-4677-1041-1 (EB pdf)
        1. Paper—Juvenile literature. 2. Papermaking—Juvenile literature. 3. Timber—Juvenile literature.
    I. Title.
    TS1105.5.M37 2013
    676—dc23   2012007921

Manufactured in the United States of America
6-42901-12711-9/12/2016

TABLE OF Contents

We **use paper every day.** How is it made?

Workers plant trees.

Most paper comes from trees. Workers plant some trees just for making paper. It takes many years for a tree to get big.

Workers cut the trees.

Workers cut down tall, thick trees. They chop off the branches to make logs. Trucks take the logs to a **paper mill**. A paper mill is a place where paper is made.

A machine takes off bark.

A paper mill is full of machines. The first machine takes bark off the logs.

The logs are chopped.

A big machine called a **chipper** crushes and grinds the logs. The logs break apart into tiny chips of wood.

The wood is washed.

Other machines wash and smash the wood chips. **Pulp** pours out. Pulp is a wet, lumpy mix of ground-up wood and water.

Water drips down.

The wet pulp pours onto a screen. The screen lets the water drip down. Long, thin threads of wood called **fibers** stay on top. The wet fibers make a long sheet of paper.

The paper is dried.

Heavy rollers squeeze more water out of the paper. Then hot rollers and ovens dry the paper.

The paper is rolled.

Machines wrap the dry paper into huge rolls. The rolls are as tall as a grown-up person.

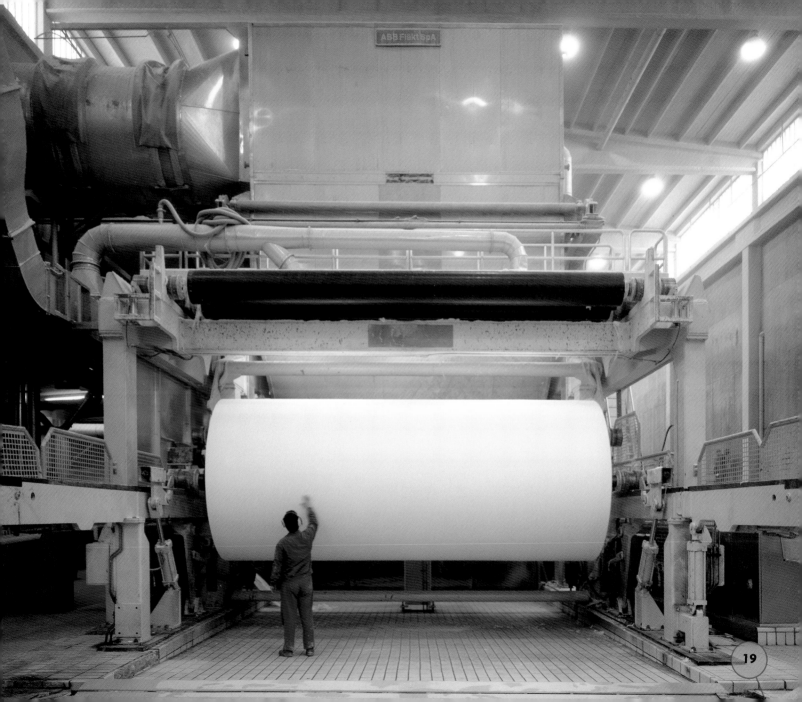

The paper is cut.

The paper is too big to be used. Workers feed it into machines that cut it. Some of the finished paper is sent to stores. Some is sent to factories for printing.

Read all about it!

Grab a printed newspaper, comic book, or magazine. All are made from paper!

Glossary

chipper (CHIP-ur): a machine that chops logs into wood chips

fibers (FYE-burz): long, thin threads of wood

paper mill (PAY-pur MILL): a place where paper is made

pulp (PUHLP): a mix of water and ground-up wood

Index

LERNER
e
SOURCE

Expand learning beyond the printed book. Download free, complementary educational resources for this book from our website, www.lernerresource.com.